.95

W9-DDQ-523

Evolution

Andres Llamas Ruiz

Illustrations by Ferrón-Retana

Sterling Publishing Co., Inc.

New York

Illustrations by Ferrón-Retana
Text by Andres Llamas Ruiz
Translated by Natalia Tizón

Library of Congress Cataloging-in-Publication Data

Llamas Ruiz, Andrés.
   [Evolución. English]
   Evolution / Andres Llamas Ruiz.
      p.   cm. — (Cycles of life)
   Includes index.
   Summary: Describes the process of evolution, beginning with single-celled organisms and culminating with the appearance of man.
   ISBN 0-8069-9329-4
   1. Evolution (Biology)—Juvenile literature. [1. Evolution.] I. Title. II. Series: Llamas Ruiz, Andrés. Secuencias de la naturaleza. English.
QH367.1.L5813   1996
575—dc20
                                            96–25863
                                                CIP
                                                AC

1 3 5 7 9 10 8 6 4 2

Published by Sterling Publishing Company, Inc.
387 Park Avenue South, New York, N.Y. 10016
Originally published in Spain by Ediciones Estes
©1996 by Ediciones Estes, S.A. ©1996 by Ediciones Lema, S.L.
English version and translation © 1996 by Sterling Publishing Company, Inc.
Distributed in Canada by Sterling Publishing
℅ Canadian Manda Group, One Atlantic Avenue, Suite 105
Toronto, Ontario, Canada M6K 3E7
Distributed in Great Britain and Europe by Cassell PLC
Wellington House, 125 Strand, London WC2R 0BB, England
Distributed in Australia by Capricorn Link (Australia) Pty Ltd.
P.O. Box 6651, Baulkham Hills, Business Centre, NSW 2153, Australia
Printed and Bound in Spain
All rights reserved

Sterling ISBN 0-8069-9329-4

Contents

Life began from single-cell organisms.

The earth was formed 4,500 million years ago. It was a ball, made up of gases and oceans of melted lava—a place where there was no life at all.

Gradually, the earth's surface cooled down and torrential rain, lasting centuries, formed primitive oceans. Here, life originated more than 4,000 million years ago.

It is very difficult to know exactly what the planet's first forms of life were like, since they were tiny and did not leave behind a record of fossilized remains.

The first known fossils were stromatolites—primitive single-cell organisms (formed of only one cell). Other microorganisms, such as bacteria, cyanobacteria, and cyanophiceous algae, developed photosynthesis (a way of using energy from the sun to create food). As time progressed, single-cell organisms learned to cooperate with each other and formed multicellular organisms (which include many cells), such as human beings.

3,800 million years: The first sedimentary rocks were formed.

3,500 million years: The first fossils (stromatolites) appeared.

2,500 million years: Cyanophiceous algae appeared.

1,500 million years: Eucaryotic cells appeared.

600 million years: The first "multicellular" animals were formed.

6

2

1

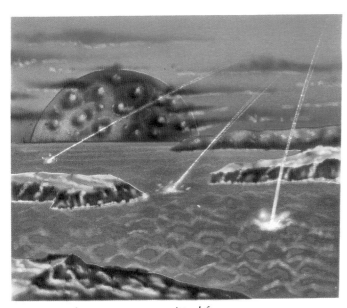

Stromatolites are round, rocky fossils that can be as small as a few inches or as big as several feet in diameter. Inside them are the remains of microorganisms more than 3,000 million years old.

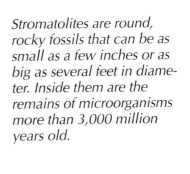

Gases and water vapor emitted from inside the earth formed giant dark, threatening clouds, which released a rainstorm that lasted for centuries. The first oceans were created in this way.

The first forms of life were very small and soft, consisting of only a few cells.

Even so, they were extremely varied.
1. Cyanoflagellum
2. Protozoa

3. Primitive sponge
4. Primitive jellyfish
5. Worm
6. Volvox

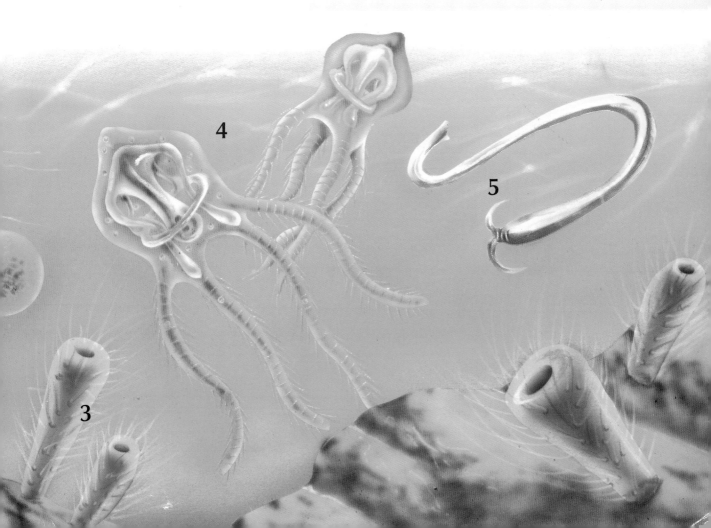

These organisms evolved to form the first fish.

Not all fish had a shell. Jamoytius, for example, had a long, narrow body with a long dorsal fin. Its mouth was round and designed for suction. It was a parasite, which fed off other fish, much like today's lamprey.

From the first appearance of life, a long time passed before a new type of creature—the vertebrate—appeared 500 million years ago. These were the first creatures known to have bones. Their features, however, were still very primitive.

They did not have jaws or teeth, and are referred to as agnostids, or jawless fish. Their system of eating was very special. They would suck nutrients found in the mud of the ocean bottom or from plankton (minute water-dwelling plants or animals). They moved clumsily and the only protection they had against their enemies was a heavy bone shell that covered their head and the front of their body. Due to this curious defense system, these fish are also called Ostracoderm, which means "shell skin."

Despite their strange appearance, their internal system was similar to present-day fish. However, their peculiar eating system did not allow them to catch big prey, which meant that most of them could grow only a few inches long.

2

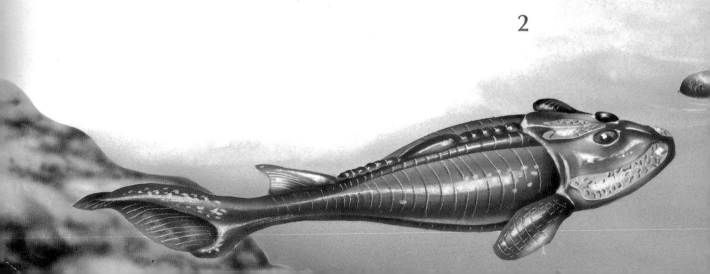

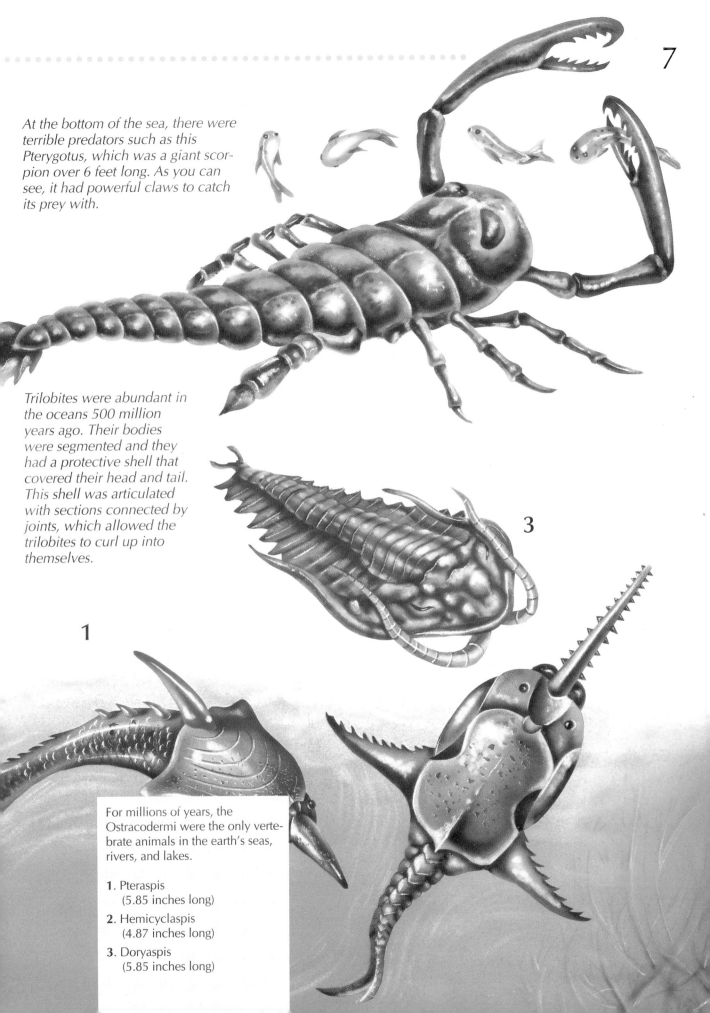

At the bottom of the sea, there were terrible predators such as this Pterygotus, which was a giant scorpion over 6 feet long. As you can see, it had powerful claws to catch its prey with.

Trilobites were abundant in the oceans 500 million years ago. Their bodies were segmented and they had a protective shell that covered their head and tail. This shell was articulated with sections connected by joints, which allowed the trilobites to curl up into themselves.

3

1

For millions of years, the Ostracodermi were the only vertebrate animals in the earth's seas, rivers, and lakes.

1. Pteraspis
   (5.85 inches long)
2. Hemicyclaspis
   (4.87 inches long)
3. Doryaspis
   (5.85 inches long)

Primitive fish evolved into fish with jaws and teeth.

Some 400 million years ago, vertebrates evolved. They "invented" a new system of eating and a movable mouth, with jaws that could open and close. These jaws had teeth, which meant that the fish did not have to rely completely on tiny plankton, animals, and nutritive particles. Fish could now catch their own prey!

Jawed animals soon dominated the others, which would eventually become extinct because they could not compete. Due to the new eating system, fish gradually increased in size and weight; they went from a few inches long to enormous sizes of over several feet in length and hundreds of pounds in weight. They became true monsters of the primitive seas.

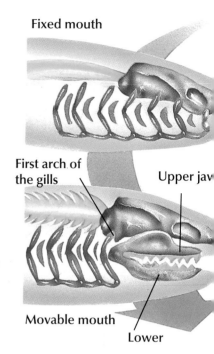

Fixed mouth

First arch of the gills

Upper jaw

Movable mouth

Lower

Jaws evolved from the first arch of the gills of jawless fish. The arch changed, forming upper and lower jaws.

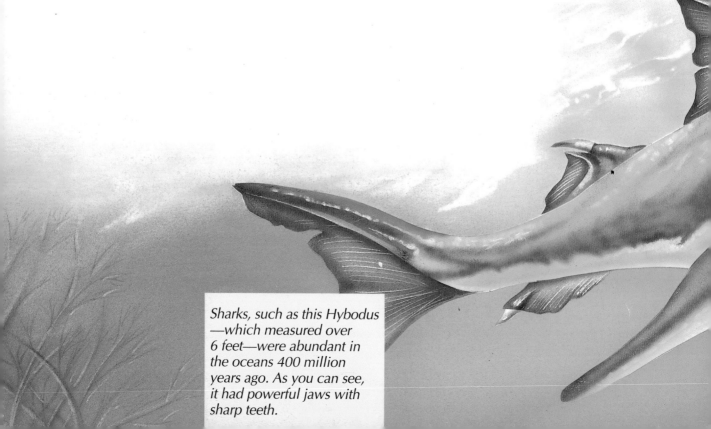

Sharks, such as this Hybodus —which measured over 6 feet—were abundant in the oceans 400 million years ago. As you can see, it had powerful jaws with sharp teeth.

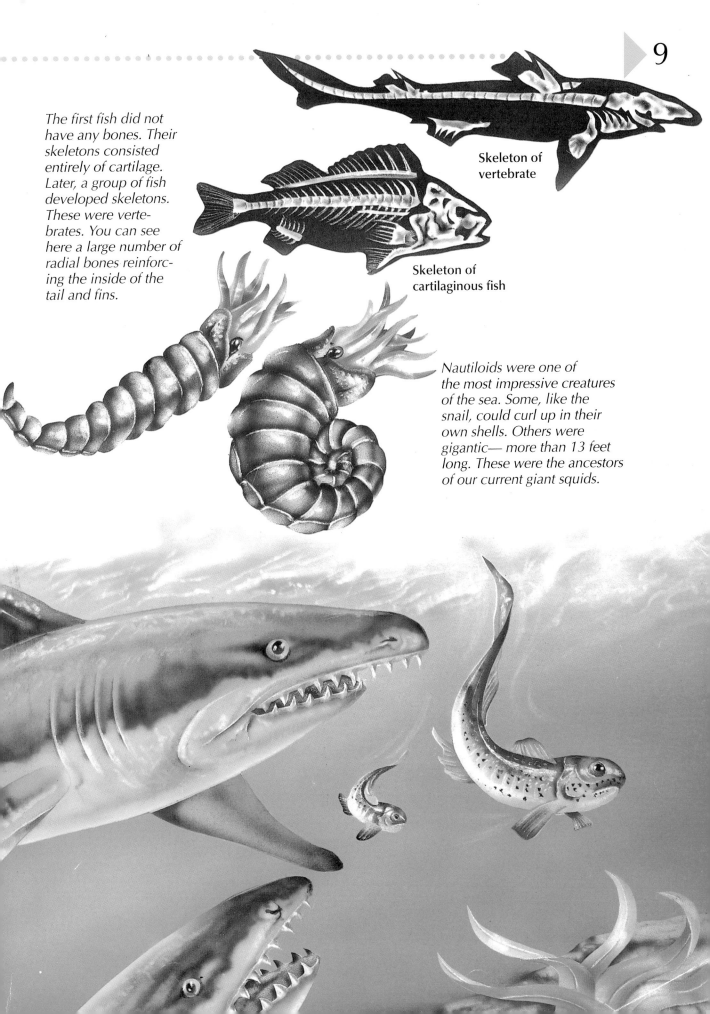

The first fish did not have any bones. Their skeletons consisted entirely of cartilage. Later, a group of fish developed skeletons. These were vertebrates. You can see here a large number of radial bones reinforcing the inside of the tail and fins.

Skeleton of vertebrate

Skeleton of cartilaginous fish

Nautiloids were one of the most impressive creatures of the sea. Some, like the snail, could curl up in their own shells. Others were gigantic— more than 13 feet long. These were the ancestors of our current giant squids.

The first vertebrates had bony fins and were able to leave the water.

A new species appeared in warm, shallow waters 400 million years ago. Their most distinct features were very strong pelvic and pectoral fins made of big, fleshy lobes that were held together by jointed bones. Later, these fins adapted to help fish move on mud, and eventually they became the support system that would carry the weight of the fish's body when it left the water.

These fish lived in warm, shallow water that might easily dry up, threatening the fish's survival. If that happened, the fins would allow the creatures to crawl along the ground to another, deeper pond. These were the first vertebrates to "walk" on land.

During times of drought, Dipnoi, which lived in both fresh- and saltwater swamps, preferred to sink down into the muddy bottom, and remain lethargic until conditions improved.

1

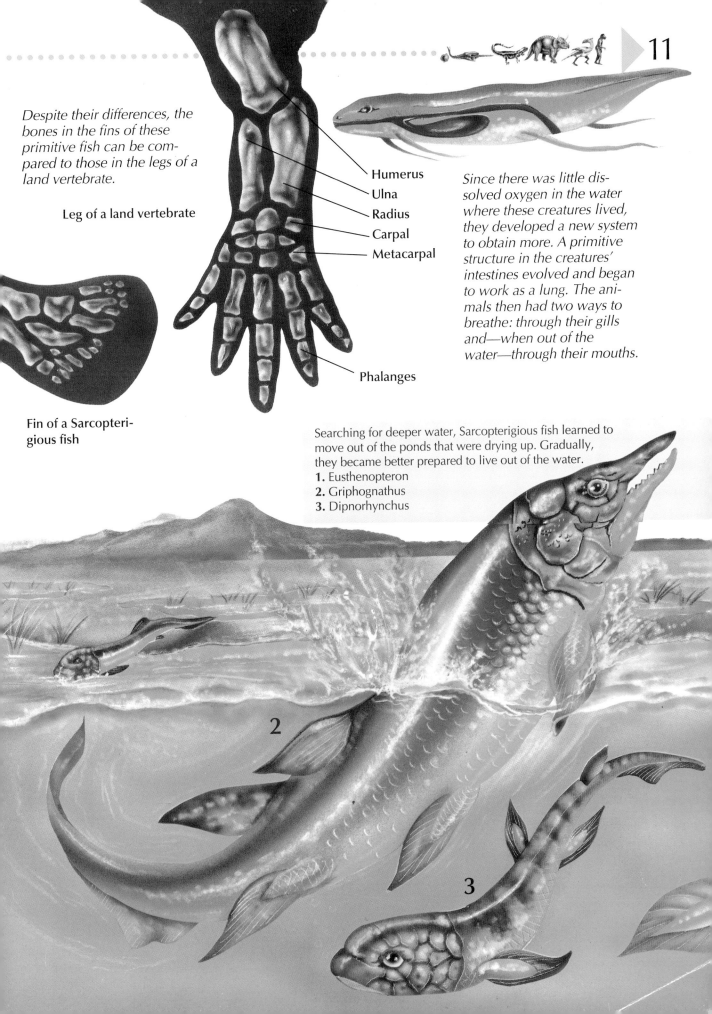

Despite their differences, the bones in the fins of these primitive fish can be compared to those in the legs of a land vertebrate.

Leg of a land vertebrate

Humerus
Ulna
Radius
Carpal
Metacarpal

Phalanges

Fin of a Sarcopterigious fish

Since there was little dissolved oxygen in the water where these creatures lived, they developed a new system to obtain more. A primitive structure in the creatures' intestines evolved and began to work as a lung. The animals then had two ways to breathe: through their gills and—when out of the water—through their mouths.

Searching for deeper water, Sarcopterigious fish learned to move out of the ponds that were drying up. Gradually, they became better prepared to live out of the water.
1. Eusthenopteron
2. Griphognathus
3. Dipnorhynchus

2

3

These became the first amphibians, which lived both in and out of water.

After a group of fish "learned" to leave the water, some of them evolved and they eventually became the first amphibians.

The first amphibians to adapt to life outside of water found a "new" world, even if they had trouble learning to travel around in it. Many of them, such as the Ichthyostega (which "walked" on land 370 million years ago), still moved rather clumsily on solid ground and preferred to stay near the water.

These amphibians had many characteristics of earlier fish, such as scales, a long tail fin, and an enormous mouth. They had four legs with toes, and they were also the first creatures with a "neck," even if it was a short one. Their spines and ribs grew much stronger, which allowed them to move out of the water.

Most of these first amphibians caught their prey under water by propelling their powerful tail fin.

This is the skeleton of the oldest known amphibian, Ichthyostega. As you can see, all the bone structures are highly reinforced.

Eye

Highly reinforced ribs

Powerful tail

Nostril

Forelegs

Strong spine

Back legs

The bodies of some amphibians changed a great deal. This Platyhyptix had a crest in order to regulate its temperature.

The first amphibians used their powerful tails to help them catch their prey under water. The most primitive ones remained near the water, and chose shallow waters as breeding grounds.

Amphibians evolved, adapting to life on solid ground.

After the first amphibians left the water, they evolved a great deal, especially during the Carboniferous period. Because they had no competition, they became successful, evolving into many shapes and reaching gigantic proportions.

In time, these new species adapted to spending most of their lives on solid ground, although they had to go back to the water to reproduce, just as frogs do today.

Each species of amphibian was very different from another. Some were only a few inches long, while others grew to be more than 13 feet tall.

Their habits were also diverse. Some were herbivores (plant eaters); others were predators.

According to one theory, after more than 65 million years of warm, humid weather—which was ideal for the lifestyle of amphibians—the climate changed and the earth then entered a very cold stage that caused many species of amphibians to become extinct. That period was followed by a very long dry, hot period.

Many amphibians could not survive these changes and they began to die out.

The first amphibian resembling the modern frog was Triadobatrachus, which was nearly 4 inches long and lived 240 million years ago.

Many scientists believe that temperatures gradually dropped 280 million years ago, which ultimately caused the extinction of a large number of primitive amphibians.

About 30 million years later, temperatures greatly increased and there was a very long dry, hot period. Those amphibians that had managed to survive the cold could not exist in the heat, and they, too, began to disappear.

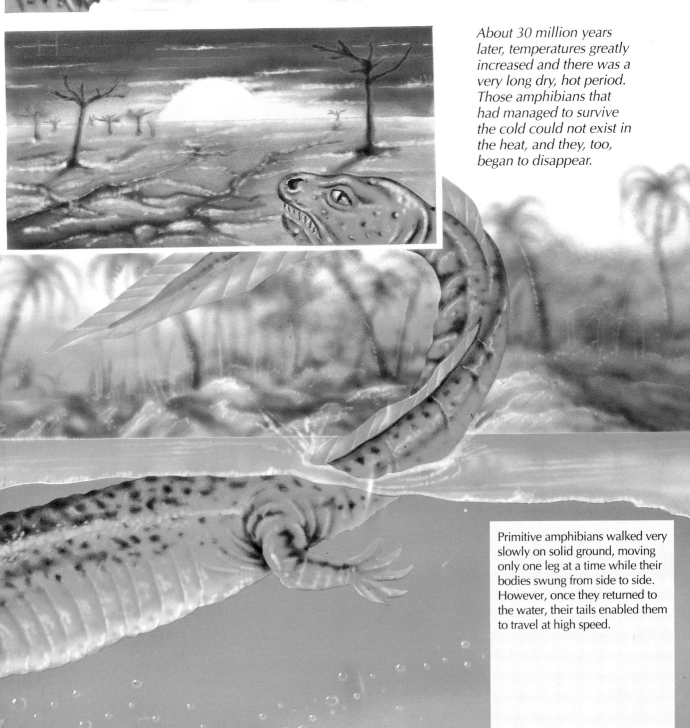

Primitive amphibians walked very slowly on solid ground, moving only one leg at a time while their bodies swung from side to side. However, once they returned to the water, their tails enabled them to travel at high speed.

From amphibians came the reptiles, the first creatures to live exclusively on land.

The first reptiles appeared 270 million years ago, at a time when, many scientists believe, the weather was still warm and humid, and amphibians dominated everywhere.

On the outskirts of the forests where the amphibians ruled, it is thought that there were areas that sometimes suffered from drought. Here, the first reptiles found their opportunity to survive, gaining independence from the water.

To live completely on land, the amphibians had to undergo a very complex transformation. The skin of the "new" reptiles was well protected to prevent water loss through evaporation. However, the most important changes came in the way the animals reproduced. Earlier, amphibians had returned to the water to breed. The reptiles were the first vertebrates to lay eggs on land. Their eggs were well protected by a hard and porous shell. Inside, an embryo was suspended in water and wrapped in a membrane.

It is believed that climate changes turned reptiles into rulers of the planet for more than 200 million years.

Menosaurus was the first reptile to return to an aquatic life. In order to breathe, it would swim up close to the water's surface. It also had large jaws filled with teeth to catch small water creatures.

Diadectes was a 12-foot-long land amphibian whose body showed a mixture of reptile and amphibian features.

The first reptiles were small. In order to survive, they had to escape far away from the humid areas where the huge amphibians lived.

The different cavities and membranes that surrounded the reptile embryo inside the egg kept it in an "aquatic" environment, even if it was far from the water.

Allantoid

Embryo

Shell

Amnium

Yolk sac

From reptiles came dinosaurs, which ruled the earth for many years.

There are many theories to explain the extinction of dinosaurs 65 million years ago. The most popular states that a huge meteorite crashed into the earth, lifting clouds of dense dust into the air, which hid the sun for months or years.

A group of reptiles started to differentiate from the others 215 million years ago. They are known as dinosaurs.

The first dinosaurs had straighter legs than other reptiles, which allowed them to stand in a more upright posture.

They moved by pushing their legs out to the side, like the lizards we are familiar with. Some dinosaurs developed their limbs so well that they could run at high speeds without needing to use their forelegs. This was extremely useful, whether they were hunting or trying to run away from their enemies!

Dinosaurs walked the earth for 150 million years. As you can guess, during this time the conditions and landscape changed. So did the dinosaurs, as they tried to adapt to an evolving world. It is not surprising then to discover that there were dinosaurs of all shapes and sizes, both herbivores and carnivores.

1

The first group of vertebrates that learned to fly were the Pterosaurs, flying reptiles that could grow to enormous sizes. This Pteranodon was about 27 feet tall.

While the dinosaurs ruled the earth's surface, the seas were ruled by enormous water reptiles, the biggest of whom were almost 50 feet long!

Dinosaurs were very different from one another. Some were more than 65 feet long, while others, such as (1) the Compsognathus, were tiny—just under 2 feet long; they weighed only about 6 pounds.

You can see here other dinosaurs, such as (2) the Stegosaurus, (3) the Apatosaurus, and (4) the Brachiosaurus.

4

3

2

During the time dinosaurs ruled the earth, birds appeared.

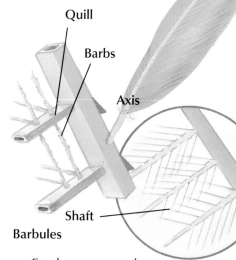

Quill

Barbs

Axis

Shaft

Barbules

The first known bird is Archaeopteryx, which appeared 150 million years ago. It had feathers, lived in trees, ate insects, and was similar in size to present-day pigeons. Because its chest muscles were still weak and its legs were big, it could not have been a very good flier. Its "flight" probably consisted of gliding gently from tree to tree with its wings and tail spread out.

In order to fly, the first birds had to undergo dramatic changes. They evolved in many ways. They grew feathers and their body weight decreased as the internal structure of their bones became lighter. Because the bone tissue of birds has small cavities full of air, the bone of a bird can weigh one-third less than the bone of a mammal!

Feathers are much more complex structures than they seem. The first feathers appeared as ragged scales in primitive reptiles, which protected them from the cold and prevented the loss of body heat. Later, they helped primitive birds to fly.

1

The bones of a bird's forelegs changed significantly to help support the wings. In addition, the sternum—or breastbone—developed a bone crest called a keel, to which the powerful muscles that moved the wing were fixed. You can see here (1) a Compsognathus, which is a small running dinosaur and an ancestor of our birds; (2) an Archaeopteryx, the first known bird; and (3) a present-day bird.

When Archaeopteryx jumped to the ground from a tree, its large, air-resistant feathers cushioned the landing. Then the bird used its claws to climb back up the tree.

2

3

Birds finally conquered the skies after the dinosaurs disappeared.

Some birds stopped flying and increased greatly in size. They no longer dominated the sky; many of them reduced the size of their wings and became running birds, with long, sturdy back legs and strong claws. Some of them became feared predators. They were very fast, and had powerful, sharp beaks, which they used to kill their prey. Between 65 and 55 million years ago, the vertebrates that dominated the earth's surface were those that evolved from non-flying birds.

Over the years, birds continued to evolve dramatically. For example, some of them adapted to live near the sea and even learned to swim and dive for fish.

The Dinorix was over 11 feet high, the tallest bird ever. It lived in New Zealand, and ate seeds and fruit until it became extinct, as a result of man's hunting.

For several millions of years, the earth's vast flat lands were dominated by giant carnivorous running birds, such as (1) Andalgalornis and (2) Phorusrhacus inflatus. In time, millions of these birds disappeared, making way for more evolved hunters, such as the jaguar and the puma.

1

Hesperornis was a sea bird, a little more than 3 feet tall, and incapable of flying. It swam with big, webbed feet and could capture such fast-moving prey as fish and squid by holding them with its long beak and sharp teeth.

Naturally, not all birds stopped flying. Some, such as this Osteodontornis, developed wings up to almost 20 feet long, which allowed it to travel great distances and glide with hardly any effort at all.

2

Mammals also increased quickly in size and number.

Birds were not the only ones evolving from reptiles.

More than 300 million years ago, a very particular group of reptiles that were similar to mammals lived in warm, humid forests. In the beginning, they were small and looked like lizards. Later, they evolved into a very different species and were much bigger and stronger, and had fearsome jaws.

These reptiles adapted in very significant ways. One feature was their ability to control their body temperature. Another was the advanced development of their skull structure and their jaw, which were key factors in their success. They evolved into insignificant creatures that looked like shrews. These were the first mammals.

Pelycosaur

Primitive therapsid

Primitive mammal

Current mammal (dog)

Many changes were necessary to transform the jaws of the primitive reptiles into current forms. As you can see, at the beginning the jaw was formed by several bones, but in the modern mammal the jaw is formed only by the dental bone.

3

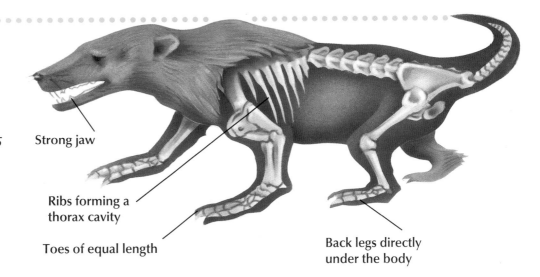

Thrinaxodon was one of the reptiles that was similar to the more advanced mammals. It was a small carnivore—only about 1.5 feet long—but it was able to run very fast. It had many characteristics of current mammals.

Strong jaw

Ribs forming a thorax cavity

Toes of equal length

Back legs directly under the body

In the Triassic period, reptiles similar to mammals were abundant and evolved into carnivores, herbivores, and insectivores. In time, they would evolve to form the first mammals. Here are some of the reptiles:

1- Kannemeyeria (up to 9 feet long) was a herbivore the size of a current ox and was well adapted to life on firm ground. Its beak-shaped mouth could take big bites out of leaves and roots.

2- Cynognathus (just over 3 feet long) was a predator with powerful jaws, molars (used to tear food), and cutting incisors (knifelike canine teeth).

3- Lystrosaurus (just over 3 feet long) lived in shallow water, eating wild water plants. It looked like a "reptilian hippopotamus."

1

2

Over millions of years, mammals experienced great anatomical changes.

When the first mammals appeared, the world was still dominated by large reptiles, especially by dinosaurs. The mammals—which were an average of 4 or 4.8 inches long—had to learn to survive in a world populated by giant creatures. However, they possessed certain anatomical features that were key to their success.

During the early stages of their evolution, most of them lived in trees and had nocturnal habits, which means they hunted and prowled at night. Even the first mammals were able to control their body temperatures; thus, they freed themselves from being dependent on outside temperatures and were able to be active for much longer periods of time.

In addition, their offspring were completely formed at birth. This was a big advantage, since mammals did not have to run the risk of having their eggs eaten or destroyed by other creatures.

Female mammals have mammary glands, which produce milk to feed their offspring in the early stages of growth. The female can also leave her young behind, well hidden in a burrow, while she goes out in search of food.

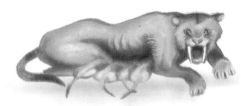

1

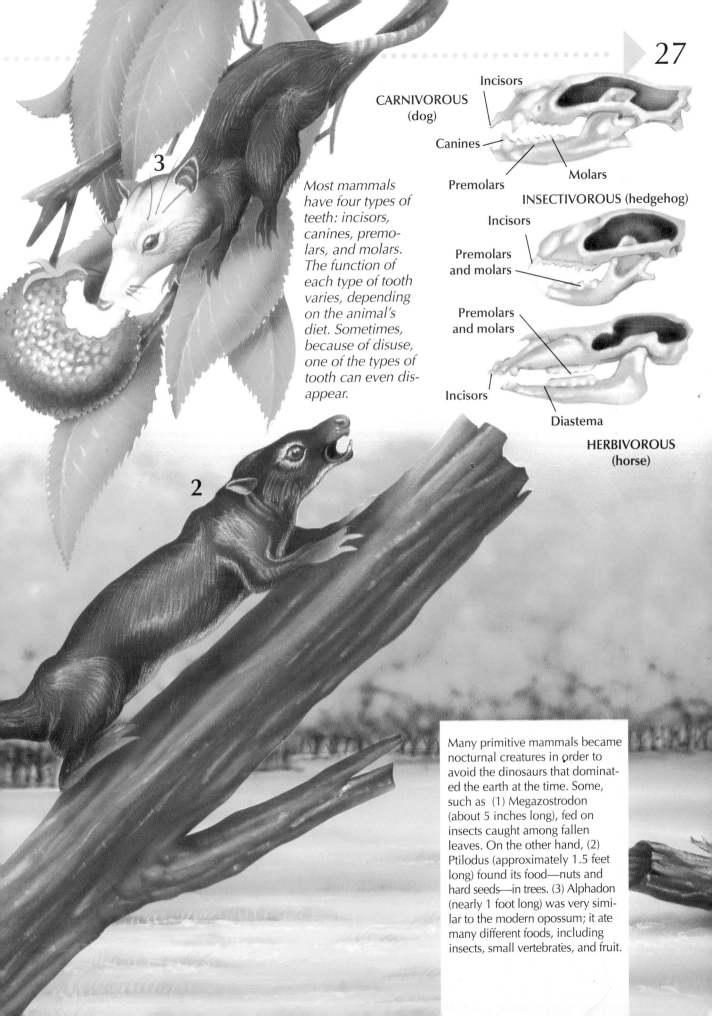

CARNIVOROUS
(dog)

Incisors

Canines

Premolars

Molars

INSECTIVOROUS (hedgehog)

Incisors

Premolars
and molars

Premolars
and molars

Incisors

Diastema

HERBIVOROUS
(horse)

Most mammals have four types of teeth: incisors, canines, premolars, and molars. The function of each type of tooth varies, depending on the animal's diet. Sometimes, because of disuse, one of the types of tooth can even disappear.

Many primitive mammals became nocturnal creatures in order to avoid the dinosaurs that dominated the earth at the time. Some, such as (1) Megazostrodon (about 5 inches long), fed on insects caught among fallen leaves. On the other hand, (2) Ptilodus (approximately 1.5 feet long) found its food—nuts and hard seeds—in trees. (3) Alphadon (nearly 1 foot long) was very similar to the modern opossum; it ate many different foods, including insects, small vertebrates, and fruit.

Mammals evolved and spread across the planet.

When the dinosaurs disappeared, mammals evolved quickly, and some millions of years later, they became the earth's dominant vertebrates.

At the end of the Cretaceous period, 65 million years ago, the earth's surface experienced a very important change. Dinosaurs disappeared. As a result, primitive mammals gradually spread out and adapted themselves to occupy all the environments that had been emptied. Since they no longer had to hide from giant enemies, they could increase in size and adopt daytime habits. Fifty million years ago, mammals—ranging from flying bats to water animals, such as dolphins and whales—had spread all over the earth.

The biggest distinctions of mammals took place 15 million years ago. Since then, the planet's climate has changed many times—especially during the great glacial eras of the last 2 million years. Those climate changes caused a reduction in the variety of mammals.

Although it still had some primitive features, Icaronycteris was very similar to the modern bat. It lived, as do its current relatives, by catching insects with its wings while flying close to the water at dusk.

1

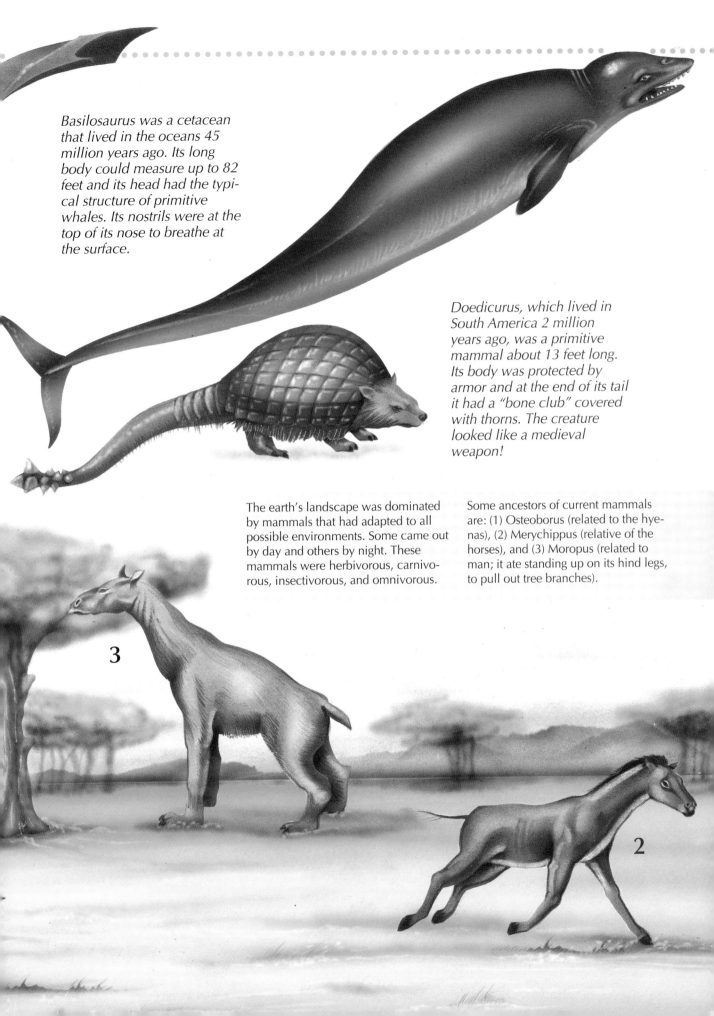

Basilosaurus was a cetacean that lived in the oceans 45 million years ago. Its long body could measure up to 82 feet and its head had the typical structure of primitive whales. Its nostrils were at the top of its nose to breathe at the surface.

Doedicurus, which lived in South America 2 million years ago, was a primitive mammal about 13 feet long. Its body was protected by armor and at the end of its tail it had a "bone club" covered with thorns. The creature looked like a medieval weapon!

The earth's landscape was dominated by mammals that had adapted to all possible environments. Some came out by day and others by night. These mammals were herbivorous, carnivorous, insectivorous, and omnivorous.

Some ancestors of current mammals are: (1) Osteoborus (related to the hyenas), (2) Merychippus (relative of the horses), and (3) Moropus (related to man; it ate standing up on its hind legs, to pull out tree branches).

The height of the evolutionary process was the appearance of man.

The process that caused the appearance of man started 5 million years ago, when a primitive hominid separated from the evolution line that would later create gorillas and chimpanzees. This first "hominid" still walked leaning on its knuckles and its brain capacity was rather small.

In Africa, a more evolved hominid appeared 4 million years ago. This was Australopithecus, whose brain measured almost 27.5 cubic inches. It could walk upright on two feet, without leaning on its hands. This characteristic was very important for the evolution of man because it allowed the creature to see above tall grass, making it possible to spot predators. It also allowed the hominids to carry objects in their hands.

Two million years ago, the first "man" appeared. This was Homo habilis, whose name comes from his capacity to use rough stone utensils.

Until very recently, the cave bear lived in Europe. In its primitive form, it was hunted by Neanderthal men, who used its bones for rituals.

1

2

3

You can see here the evolutionary sequence from hominid to modern man:

1-Ramapithecus (4 feet tall). He lived 15 million years ago.

2- Australopithecus (4 feet tall). He lived 3.5 million years ago, had a brain capacity of almost 27.5 cubic inches, and could walk on two feet.

3-Homo habilis (4 to 5 feet tall). He lived 2 to 1.5 million years ago, had a brain capacity of almost 49 cubic inches, and was probably able to "speak." He could make some small stone tools.

4-Homo erectus (5.5 feet tall). He lived 1.6 million years ago and had a brain capacity of between 58 and 73 cubic inches. He traveled and hunted in groups and made tools, such as spears and knives from wood, stone, horn, and bone.

5-Homo sapiens neanderthalensis (5.5 feet tall). The "Neanderthal man" evolved more than 200,000 years ago and disappeared 30,000 years ago. His features and brain were very similar to today's humans.

6-Homo sapiens sapiens. Current man.

The first hominids had to live with huge mammals, such as this mammoth of the plains (almost 15 feet tall). Its tusks were more than 16 feet long!

Glossary

Bacteria: Single-cell microorganism that can be of many different types. Some of them are useful for agriculture, some cause diseases, others take part in fermentation and putrefaction processes, and etc.

Carnivore: An animal whose diet is based on flesh.

Cartilaginous tissue: The tissue of the organism that reinforces its body structure. It is more flexible than bone tissue.

Fossil: The remains or impression of an organism of past geological ages that has been preserved in the earth's crust.

Gills: Respiratory organ of the fish.

Through them, fish obtain the necessary oxygen to live from the water.

Herbivore: An animal whose diet is based on grass, plants, etc.

Keel: The outstanding and sharp part of the birds' sternum. It is where the pectoral muscles are fixed in order to move the wings while flying.

Photosynthesis: The process in which green plants compose organic matter from carbon dioxide by using light as a source of energy.

Predator: An animal that watches and attacks other animals in order to eat.

Stromatolites: The oldest known fossils of living organisms.

Vertebrate: An animal that has bone or cartilaginous internal skeleton.

Index